WELCOME ADVENTURER!

YOU ARE ABOUT TO SET OFF ON A JOURNEY THAT WILL TAKE YOU THROUGH DIFFERENT HABITATS ON EARTH AND EVEN INTO OUTER SPACE!

Each page in this book has different fun facts to find. Here's how it works:

① Look for the 'start here' icon, this is where you start!

START HERE

② There is a list of things to find on each page, use your finger to follow the path and find them!

things to find:
Starfish
Crab
Turtle
Octopus
Seahorse
Shark
Whale
Jellyfish

③ Enjoy learning all the fun facts in this book!

OCEAN DISCOVERY

Animals to find:
Starfish
Crab
Turtle
Octopus
Seahorse
Shark
Whale
Jellyfish

START HERE

Turtle
Turtles date back to the time of the dinosaurs, over 200 million years ago!

Octopus
Some octopuses can shoot ink from thier bodies if they get attacked!

Whale
A blue whale is the largest animal to have ever lived on planet Earth!

Starfish
Did you know that there is over 1600 species of starfish, and they eat oysters and snails!

Clown Fish
Did you know – All clownfish are born boys, but some turn into girls in later life?

Shark
A shark's teeth are usually replaced every 8 days!

Crab
Crabs belong to a group of animals called Decapods, meaning they have 10 legs!

Seahorse
Did you know? Seahorses prefer to swim in pairs with their tails linked together!

Jellyfish
Jellyfish have no brain, heart, bones or eyes!

Tractor
A tractor is the most important vehicle on a farm and can pull many different tools or trailers

Bull
Bulls can't actually see red or green as they are colorblind!

Scarecrow
The first scarecrows were used over 3000 years ago!

Pig
Pigs are intelligent animals and have an excellent sense of smell!

Duck
Ducks webbed feet do not feel the cold as they do not have nerves or blood vessels in them!

Jupiter
Jupiter is the largest planet in our solar system. It is 318 times bigger than Earth!

Saturn
Saturn is the second largest planet in our solar system, and it's rings are made of ice!

Things to find:
Jupiter
Mars
Earth
The Sun
Shooting Star
Saturn
The Moon

START HERE

SPACE ADVENTURE

The Moon

The moon is responsible for the tides in the ocean on Earth!

Mars

Mars is known as the red planet. One year on Mars lasts 687 Earth days!

Earth

Around 71% of Earth's surface is covered in water and only 29% is covered in land!

Shooting Star

Scientists study shooting stars to predict the weather and understand the atmosphere.

the Sun

In the centre of our solar system, the sun is the most important source of energy for life on Earth. It is 109 times bigger than Earth!

BUG HUNTING

things to find:
Grasshopper
Snail
Butterfly
Dragonfly
Bumble Bee
Caterpillar
Ant
Spider

START HERE

Butterfly
Butterflies have taste buds on their feet!

Grasshopper
Grasshoppers make noise by rubbing their legs together!

Snail
Some snails live on land and in water!

Dragonfly
Dragonflies eat other bugs!

Bumbe Bee
Male bumble bees cannot sting as they do not have a stinger!

Spider
Spiders are not actually insects! Insects have 6 legs but spiders have 8 legs.

Caterpillar
A caterpillar grows wings and becomes a butterfly!

Ant
A single ant can carry up to 50 times it's own body weight!

A JUNGLE ADVENTURE

START HERE

things to find:
Tiger
Hippo
Lemur
Panda
Monkey
Leopard
Crocodile
Flamingo

Flamingo
Flamingos are pink because the food they eat turns their feathers pink!

Crocodile
Crocodiles have the strongest bite of any animal in the world

Panda
Panda paws have 5 fingers and a bone coming out of it's wrist which it uses like a thumb!

Leopard
Leopards hunt at night and can carry their food up into the trees!

Monkey
Marmoset monkeys have longer tails than their bodies!

Lemur
Lemurs have a scent gland in their tails and they have 'stink' fights!

Hippo
A Hippopotamus can hold it's breath for over 5 minutes!

Tiger
Tigers are the biggest cats in the world and are very good swimmers!

DINOSAUR SPOTTING

Things to find:
Stegosaurus
Triceratops
Oloritan
Prenocephale
Brontosaurus
Pteranodon
Tyrannosaur

START HERE

Oloritan
Known as a duck billed dinosaur

Stegosaurus
Did you know – Stegosaurus had a brain the size of a ping pong ball!

Triceratops
Triceratops had one of the largest heads of any land animal – and up to 800 teeth!

Pteranodon
A flying dinosaur who loved to eat fish!

Tyrannosaur
Known as T-Rex, this dinosaur had the largest teeth of all the dinosaurs!

Prenocephale
The domed head of this dinosaur made it look very silly!

Brontosaurus
One of the largest dinosaurs, but it wasn't very clever as it had a small head and brain!

ARCTIC EXPLORER

things to find:
Killer Whale
Arctic Fox
Walrus
Eskimo
Polar Bear
Moose
Narwhal
Penguin

START HERE

Killer Whale
Killer whales are actually the largest Dolphins in the sea, they are only called whales because of their huge size!

Arctic Fox
Arctic foxes fur is brown in the summer and white in the winter! They are only the size of a house cat!

Penguin
No penguins live at the North Pole, and even though they have wings they can't fly!

Narwhal
A Narwhal is a whale which has a huge horn which is growing from one of it's teeth!

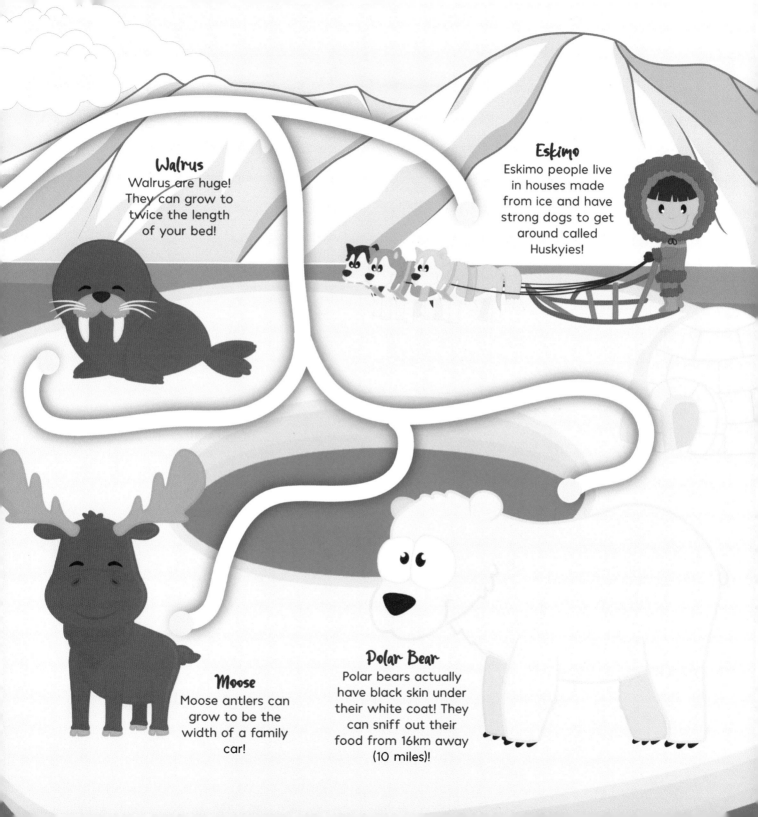

Walrus
Walrus are huge! They can grow to twice the length of your bed!

Eskimo
Eskimo people live in houses made from ice and have strong dogs to get around called Huskyies!

Moose
Moose antlers can grow to be the width of a family car!

Polar Bear
Polar bears actually have black skin under their white coat! They can sniff out their food from 16km away (10 miles)!

BIRD SPOTTING

START HERE

things to find:
Toucan
Ostrich
Eagle
Stork
Parrot
Vulture
Peacock

Toucan
A toucan beak is one third of its body size, and it's made of keratin, which is like human hair.

Eagle
The bald eagle takes its name from the fact it's head is white and the rest of it's body is brown!

Ostrich
The Ostrich is the world's largest bird and stands taller than a man at up to 9 feet tall!

Stork
A Stork doesn't sing like most other birds, it is almost voiceless and largely silent!

Parrot
Parrots are believed to be one of the most intelligent of all birds, some species even imitate human voices!

Vulture
Vultures do not hunt their own food. Instead, they eat other animals left overs!

Peacock
Peacocks have beautiful tails, but they weigh quite heavy so they can't fly very far!

Mount Rushmore
A famous landmark in America. Dynamite was used to carve the faces into Mount Rushmore!

Statue of Liberty
There are 354 steps to climb inside the statue and she has a size 879 shoe!

START HERE

AROUND THE WORLD

things to find:
Christ the Redeemer
Mount Rushmore
Statue of Liberty
Taj Mahal
Sydney Opera House
Leaning Tower of Pisa
Great Wall of China

Christ the Redeemer
The statue of Jesus Christ overlooks Rio de Janeiro in Brazil, and stands on top of a huge mountain!

Leaning Tower of Pisa

This tower in Italy took 199 years to build and it is leaning because one side of it is slowly sinking!

Great Wall of China

The Great Wall is the longest structure ever built by humans and can be seen from space!

Taj Mahal

It took around 20 years to build this fabulous building in India, it is made of white marble!

Sydney Opera House

Australia's famous opera house, the design of which was the result of a competition held in 1956!

SAFARI ADVENTURE

Things to find:
Water Buffalo
Gazelle
Zebra
Elephant
Hyena
Rhino
Giraffe
Lion

Water buffalo
Water buffalo have unusual shaped horns to protect themselves against predators.

Zebra
A zebra's stripes are like our fingerprints – no two are the same!

Elephant
Elephants are the largest land animal in the world, and have incredible memories!

Hyena
A hyena laughing? This is how they communicate with each other!

Gazelle
Gazelles are extremely fast animals and can jump really far!

Rhino
A rhinoceros horn is not made of bone, it is actually made of the same substance as hair and fingernails!

Lion
A lion's roar can be heard up to 8km away (5 miles)!

Giraffe
A giraffes neck is too short to reach the ground so they have to spread their legs to drink!

WOODLAND WONDERS

START HERE

things to find:
Bear
Fox
Hedgehog
Wild Boar
Owl
Deer
Hare

Owl
Owls are farsighted, meaning they can't see things close to their eyes clearly!

Wild Boar
Until the 1930's, the hair of a wild boar was often used to make toothbrushes!

Fox
A fox is in fact the smallest member of the dog family!

Hedgehog
Hedgehog spines are like our teeth! They have a baby set and shed them for an adult set!

Hare
Hare's can run very fast, up to 72kph (45mph)! They are also larger than rabbits and have longer ears

Deer
Most deer are born with white spots on their back but lose them within a year.

Bear
There is 8 species of bear in the world, and they all have 2 layers of fur!

GETTING AROUND

START HERE

Things to find:
- Train
- Car
- Bus
- Helicopter
- Hot Air Balloon
- Submarine
- Monster Truck
- Sail Boat

Monster Truck
Monster trucks can do stunts, including front and back wheelies!

Bus
The world's largest bus is in China and it carries up to 300 people!

21 LONDON BRIDGE
LONDON

Car
The first modern motor car was built in 1886 by a German man called Carl Benz.

Train
Early trains relied on ropes, horses or gravity!

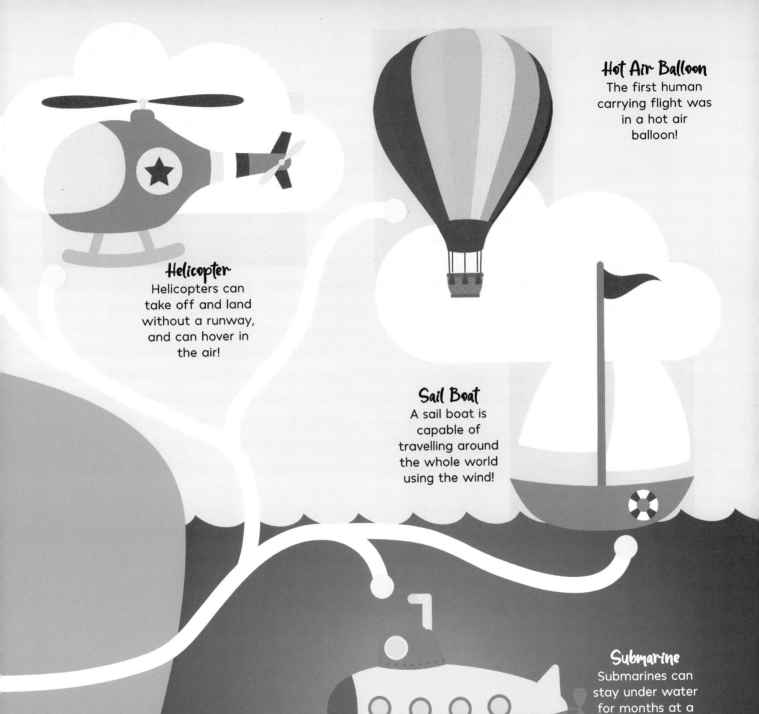

Hot Air Balloon
The first human carrying flight was in a hot air balloon!

Helicopter
Helicopters can take off and land without a runway, and can hover in the air!

Sail Boat
A sail boat is capable of travelling around the whole world using the wind!

Submarine
Submarines can stay under water for months at a time!

Badger
Badgers are surprisingly fast! They can run 30km per hour (nearly 20mph)!

Field Mouse
Mice have very poor eyesight, but make up for this with very good hearing and smell.

Squirrel
Squirrels can't fly, but they have webbing between their legs enabling them to glide between trees!

Otter
Otters are playful animals, some make waterslides to slide down into the water!

Mole
Moles love to dig and have shovel shaped front paws to help them dig fast!

DOWN BY THE RIVER

START HERE

Things to find:
Kingfisher
Frog
Field Mouse
Otter
Badger
Squirrel
Mole

Kingfisher
Kingfishers can hover above water when it searches for food!

Frog
Instead of drinking water, frogs soak it in their body through their skin!

WELL DONE! YOU HAVE COMPLETED YOUR ADVENTURE! NOW SEE IF YOU CAN REMEMBER SOME OF THE FUN FACTS YOU DISCOVERED ABOUT THE ITEMS BELOW!

Printed in Great Britain
by Amazon